Cooking with Mustard

Empowering Your Palate

G. Poggenpohl

Schiffer Publishing Ltd

4880 Lower Valley Road, Atglen, Pennsylvania 19310

Other Schiffer Books By The Author:

Cooking Together: Having Fun with Two or More Cooks in the Kitchen, 978-0-7643-3647-8, $19.99

Cooking Wild Game: Thirty-Six Hearty Dishes, 978-0-7643-3646-1, $19.99

Other Schiffer Books on Related Subjects:

Today I Cook: A Man's Guide to the Kitchen, 978-0-7643-3644-7, $19.99

Creative Ideas for Garnishing & Decorating, 978-0-7643-3645-4, $19.99

Asparagus & Strawberries, 978-0-7643-3648-5, $19.99

Schiffer Books are available at special discounts for bulk purchases for sales promotions or premiums. Special editions, including personalized covers, corporate imprints, and excerpts can be created in large quantities for special needs. For more information contact the publisher:

Published by Schiffer Publishing Ltd.
4880 Lower Valley Road
Atglen, PA 19310
Phone: (610) 593-1777; Fax: (610) 593-2002
E-mail: Info@schifferbooks.com

For the largest selection of fine reference books on this and related subjects, please visit our web site at **www.schifferbooks.com**
We are always looking for people to write books on new and related subjects. If you have an idea for a book please contact us at the above address.

This book may be purchased from the publisher. Include $5.00 for shipping. Please try your bookstore first. You may write for a free catalog.

In Europe, Schiffer books are distributed by
Bushwood Books
6 Marksbury Ave.
Kew Gardens
Surrey TW9 4JF England
Phone: 44 (0) 20 8392 8585; Fax: 44 (0) 20 8392 9876
E-mail: info@bushwoodbooks.co.uk
Website: www.bushwoodbooks.co.uk

Originally published as *Mit Senf aromatisch kochen* by EDITION XXL GmbH

Translated from the German by Dr. Edward Force
Kitchen and Photos: G. Poggenpohl, Wismar
Food styling: Caterina Marx
Layout: Mathias Weil
Typesetting: Henrik Stuerzebecher

Library of Congress Control Number: 2010939818

Type set in Avenir
ISBN: 978-0-7643-3643-0
Printed in China

COOKING with MUSTARD
EMPOWERING YOUR PALATE

Foreword

When my publisher called me and suggested I write a mustard cookbook, my first thought was: "What!? A whole cookbook with mustard?" Now that the book is finished, I can say: "You sure can cook with mustard!"

Just making mustard itself is a special subject. In fact, there so many possible variations that one could write a book just about making mustard—not to mention the many recipes in which whole mustard seeds, mustard meal, mustard paste, and mustard pickles are used. I did not anticipate such a variety. But one never runs out of things to learn.

When you consider that mustard makes foods considerably easier to digest, you will agree that a tablespoon of mustard belongs in almost every dish. Even hard-to-digest foods like cucumbers, tomatoes, legumes, meat, and fatty fish are easier to digest with mustard.

So, wander into the world of mustard with me, enjoy exciting tastes, and even some spicy recipes. I am sure you will find recipes that you will absolutely love to thrill your family and friends with.

Yours,
G. Poggenpohl

Contents

Introduction

There are various types of mustard; they all belong to the Cruciferae family. Three types in particular are used as spices. The plants are annuals and grow between 31 inches (80cm) and 8 feet (2 1/2m) tall. From the small yellow flowers classified as umbellate, 1 1/8-inch (3cm) pods containing two or three round seeds develop. The seeds of black mustard are dark brown to black, the seeds of white mustard yellowish-white, and those of Sarepta mustard from India are reddish-purple to brown.

Very early in history, man discovered mustard as a spice and a medicine. He discovered that crushed mustard meal mixed with vinegar and water made a spicy mustard paste. Interestingly enough, a whole mustard seed by itself does not taste spicy; it is only when one chews the seed up that saliva releases the enzyme myrosinase and thus the spiciness.

Mustard loses its spiciness very quickly. If it is stored at a warm temperature, the rate at which the spiciness is lost increases. For example, storing mustard at room temperature for three months reduces mustard to a spiciness below medium. Be sure to keep mustard as cool as possible. Since mustard is so heat-sensitive, you should use a spicy mustard when cooking—it will become much milder when cooked.

Does mustard make you stupid? Here one can clearly say, "NO!" This tale is based on false information. Science often offers concepts that should not be taken literally, for example, cyanogenic mustard oils. This poisonous substance, which forms a blue acid, can damage our brains permanently. But cyanogenic mustard oils never occur in mustard! The mustard oils present in mustard have positive, stimulating properties; they promote the flow of saliva, the production of stomach juices, and thus aid our digestion. Fatty foods become much more digestible thanks to mustard.

While working on this book I found that it is not at all that easy to obtain mustard meal! Basically, I had to grind white mustard seeds in a coffee grinder by myself. The same is true of black mustard seeds. I could only find these seeds at an herb stand at the farmers market and an old school pharmacy. Thus, in the recipes I have only used the more ubiquitous white mustard seeds and its meal.

I can only recommend that you make your own mustard. It tastes many times better than what you buy. I have also noticed that when using store-bought mustard in cooking, the food tastes very salty.

Making normal mustard paste is very simple and can be done quickly. Also, it will last a long time in the refrigerator. Naturally, you can also make very extravagant mustard, which requires more time to make. You can vary the taste of mustard with liquids like wine, beer, various juices, stocks, and specially produced blends. But additional ingredients like garlic, herbs, nuts, fruits, or other spices also give the mustard a new taste.

In England, homemade mustard has been a custom for many years. There are also a great many mustard mixtures commercially available there. Some of these ready-made mustard mixtures are probably available at your grocery store. A gourmet or specialty food shop may have an even larger variety.

Making Mustard Yourself

Coarse Mustard with Whole Seeds

Ingredients

2/3 cup (100g) white mustard seeds
1 tsp white mustard meal
3/8 cup (100ml) white wine vinegar
3 1/3 Tbsp (50ml) dry white wine
1 Tbsp olive oil
1 shallot
1 Tbsp honey
1 Tbsp sea salt

Preparation

1. Put the mustard seeds in a bowl, pour the white wine and white wine vinegar over them, and let stand for about 24 hours.

2. The next day, peel the shallot and chop it fine. Mix the shallot, mustard meal, sea salt, and honey. Add this mixture to the mustard seeds and mix everything.

3. A mushy mass should result. Finally, stir in the olive oil.

In a closed jar this mustard will last up to six months.

Coarse Mustard with Honey (Sweet Mustard)

Ingredients

2/3 cup (100g) white mustard seeds
1 tsp white mustard meal
3/8 cup (100ml) white wine vinegar
3 1/3 Tbsp (50ml) lively white wine
(i.e. a chardonnay or white pinot noir)

1 shallot
3 Tbsp creamy honey
1 Tbsp brown sugar
1 Tbsp sea salt

Preparation

1. Put the mustard seeds in a bowl, pour the white wine and white wine vinegar over them, and let stand about 24 hours.

2. The next day, peel the shallot and chop it fine. Mix the shallot, mustard meal, sea salt, sugar, and honey. Add the mixture to the mustard seeds and mix everything.

3. Pulverize the material coarsely with a hand mixer, making a mushy mass.

In a closed jar this mustard will last up to six months.

Making Mustard Yourself

Fine Mustard

Ingredients

2/3 cup (100g) white mustard seeds
2/3 cup (150ml) white grape juice
3 1/3 Tbsp (50ml) light vinegar
1 Tbsp oil
1 Tbsp sea salt

Preparation

1. Run the mustard seeds through a spice grinder twice and sift through a fine sieve.

2. Scatter the mustard meal in a bowl and add the grape juice, vinegar, oil, and salt; stir to a smooth, creamy mixture.

If the mustard is too firm, add a little grape juice to it.

Medium Spicy Mustard

Ingredients

- 2/3 cup (100g) white mustard seeds
- 2/3 cup (150ml) white wine vinegar
- 3 1/3 Tbsp (50ml) water
- 1 Tbsp brown sugar
- 1 tsp sea salt
- 1 clove
- 1 bay leaf
- 4 allspice berries
- 1 onion
- 2 cloves garlic
- 1 Tbsp olive oil

Preparation

1. Grind the mustard in a spice grinder. Peel and dice the onion and the garlic cloves. Crush the allspice.

2. Heat the oil in a pot and sauté the onion and garlic. Sprinkle on the sugar and let it melt. Pour the white wine vinegar and water in. Add the spices, except for the mustard meal, and bring everything to a boil.

3. Let it cook over medium heat for 8-10 minutes. Then pour the liquid through a sieve into a bowl and mix in the mustard meal. It should have a creamy consistency.

Put in jars, the mustard will last about six months.

Mustard Variations

Ramps Mustard

2/3 cup (100g) white mustard seeds
1 Tbsp (10g) black mustard seeds
3 bunches ramps (wild leeks)
1 tsp ground ginger
1/3 cup (70g) sugar
1/2 tsp salt
2/3 cup (150ml) white wine vinegar
3/8 cup (100ml) white wine

1. Grind the mustard seeds fine. Wash the ramps and chop fine. Add the ginger, sugar, and salt to the mustard meal.

2. Boil the vinegar and the wine and pour the boiling liquid in with the mustard mix, stirring. Then mix in the ramps.

3. Put the mustard in jars and let it settle about two weeks.

German Mustard

2/3 cup (100g) white mustard seeds
1/2 tsp sea salt
1 1/3 Tbsp (10g) ground cinnamon
7/8 Tbsp (5g) ground cloves
1/2 cup (100g) sugar
~1 cup (250ml) plain vinegar

1. Grind the mustard seeds and sift them. Mix all the ingredients and pour on the vinegar, making a paste.

2. Let the whole thing settle a bit until the mustard meal swells. You may need to add some liquid to it.

Düsseldorf Mustard

1/3 cup (50g) black mustard seeds
2/3 cup (100g) white mustard seeds
7/8 cup (200ml) boiling water
3 1/3 Tbsp (50ml) wine vinegar
7/8 Tbsp (5g) ground cinnamon
1/2 Tbsp (3g) ground cloves
1/2 cup (100g) sugar
3/8 cup (100ml) white wine

Grind and sift the mustard. Mix all the ingredients and put in jars.

French Mustard

2/3 cup (100g) white mustard seeds
2/3 cup (150ml) dry white wine
1/2 cup (100g) sugar
1 Tbsp (10g) grated lemon zest
1 2/3 Tbsp (10g) ground cloves
1/3 Tbsp (3g) ground ginger
1/3 tsp (1g) vanilla powder

Grind and sift the mustard. Heat the wine and dissolve the sugar in it. Mix all the ingredients and add the wine when it is still hot.

If the mustard becomes too thick, stir in a little more wine vinegar or dry wine.

French Mustard (Le Normand's)

2/3 cup (100g) white mustard seeds
1/3 cup (15g) fresh parsley
1/3 cup (15g) fresh chervil
1/3 cup (15g) fresh tarragon
1/8 cup (15g) fresh celery
1 onion
1 clove garlic
12 anchovy fillets
2/3 cup (150ml) cider
Some vinegar

1. Steam the herbs, shake dry, and chop coarsely. Peel the onion, garlic, and celery.

2. Chop all the ingredients in a blender. Grind the mustard and mix with the cider and other ingredients. Put the finished mustard in jars and cover with some vinegar.

Cider Mustard

2/3 cup (100g) white mustard seeds
1/8 cup (20g) black mustard seeds
1 knife point each ground cardamom, nutmeg, cloves, cinnamon, and ginger
1/3 cup (100g) horseradish root
4 cups (1l) grape cider
1/4 cup (50g) sugar

1. Peel and grate the horseradish fine. Cook the grape cider down to half its volume with the sugar, spices, and horseradish.

2. Grind and sift the mustard seeds. Strain the grape cider reduction and mix with the mustard meal.

Mustard Variations

Honey Mustard

2/3 cup (100g) white mustard seeds
1/8 cup (40g) honey (a creamy type)
1 Tbsp sunflower oil
1 tsp vegetable vinegar
1 pinch salt
Hot water

Grind the mustard, sift it, and then mix with the honey, sunflower oil, vinegar, and salt. If the mixture is too firm, stir in some hot water to get the right consistency.

Put the finished mustard in jars. It can be kept in the refrigerator four months.

Herb Mustard

Enough for about three jelly glasses:
1 onion and 2 cloves garlic
1 bay leaf
1 Tbsp each fresh marjoram, sage, thyme, and tarragon
2 cups (500ml) white wine vinegar
3/8 cup (100ml) water
3 cups (350g) white mustard meal
3 Tbsp brown sugar
1/2 tsp ground clove
1/2 tsp ground cinnamon
1/2 tsp ground coriander

1. Peel the onion and dice it fine. Peel the garlic, quarter, and put in a porcelain bowl with the bay leaf, marjoram, sage, thyme, and tarragon. Pour the white wine vinegar over it. Add the mustard meal, sugar, ground clove, cinnamon, and coriander and let it develop into a creamy consistency.

2. Put the mustard in screw-top jars. Before using, store in a cool area for a month while the mustard develops its full flavor.

Jesuit Mustard

6 anchovies
1/3 cup (50g) capers
2 cups (500ml) wine vinegar
2 1/2 cups (300g) white mustard meal

Chop the anchovies and capers fine and press them into a paste. Cook the vinegar and stir in the mustard meal. Let it steep a little, then stir in the anchovy-caper paste.

Horseradish Mustard

1 3/4 cups (200g) white mustard meal
7/8 cup (200ml) herbal wine vinegar
7/8 cup (200ml) water
1 horseradish root
2 apples
1 Tbsp lemon juice
3 Tbsp sugar
1 tsp salt

1. Bring the water and vinegar to a boil briefly and stir in the mustard meal. When it is all mixed, let it cool.

2. Then add peeled, finely grated horseradish root, the peeled and grated apples, and the other ingredients.

3. Mix it all well and put it in jars.

Orange Pepper Mustard

1 3/4 cups (200g) white mustard meal
7/8 cup (200ml) herbal wine vinegar
3/8 cup (100ml) water
5 Tbsp orange marmalade
1 grated orange peel
1 tsp lemon juice
2 Tbsp green peppercorns
1 tsp salt
3 Tbsp cognac
4 Tbsp sunflower oil

1. Mix all the ingredients, except the sunflower oil and cognac. Let it stand open overnight.

2. The next day, add the oil and cognac, stir everything thoroughly again, and put the mustard in jars.

Paprika Mustard

1 3/4 cups (200g) white mustard meal
7/8 cup (200ml) herbal wine vinegar
7/8 cup (200ml) water
2 tsp sweet paprika
6 Tbsp honey
3 Tbsp sherry
3 Tbsp sunflower oil

1. Boil the vinegar and water. Pour the liquid over the mustard meal, stir, and let sit for awhile.

2. Then add the other ingredients, mix well, and put in jars.

Ground Mustard Sauces

Ingredients

2 cups (500ml) milk
1 Tbsp white mustard seeds
1 onion
2 juniper berries
1 bay leaf
1 clove
1 1/3 Tbsp (20g) butter
1/4 cup (20g) flour
3 Tbsp medium spicy mustard
Salt and pepper

Preparation

1. Grind the mustard seeds.
2. Peel the onion and cut into rings.
3. Crush the juniper berries.
4. Heat the milk in a pot, add the mustard meal, onion, juniper berries, and clove, bring to a boil briefly then let it steep for about 15 minutes just under the boiling point. Then pour the milk mixture through a fine sieve into a bowl.
5. Melt the butter in a pot, sprinkle in the flour, and warm it. Stir in the spiced milk, bring to a boil, and flavor with the mustard, salt, and pepper.

This sauce is a great accompaniment for fish and meat dishes.

Delicate Mustard Sauce

Ground Mustard Sauces

Ingredients

1 1/3 Tbsp (20g) butter
1/4 cup (20g) flour
2 cups (500ml) stock
1 Tbsp medium spicy mustard
1 Tbsp spicy mustard
Salt and pepper

Preparation

1. Melt the butter in a pot, sprinkle in the flour, and warm it. Stir in the stock, bring to a boil, and flavor with the mustard, salt, and pepper.

2. Use different types of stock—chicken, fish, meat, or vegetable—as you wish to make variations of this basic mustard sauce. Also, you can give the sauce a unique flavor by adding different ingredients like chives, dill, and fresh or preserved peppercorns.

This strong mustard sauce goes well with vegetables, eggs, fish, meat, etc.

Ground Mustard Sauce

Recipes with Prepared Mustard

Ingredients

1/2 lb (200g) smoked salmon
1 2/3 cup (200g) zucchini, chopped
2 carrots
1 leek
1/2 lb (200g) potatoes
2 Tbsp butter
3 1/8 cups (750ml) chicken stock
2/3 cup (150ml) dry white wine
2 Tbsp crème fraîche
1 tsp mustard meal
2 Tbsp medium spicy mustard
Nutmeg
Salt and pepper

Preparation

1. Wash the zucchini and clean and peel the carrots. Clean the leek, halve it lengthwise and wash well under running water. Peel the potatoes and cut into cubes. Dice the other vegetables small.

2. Melt the butter in a pot and brown the vegetables. Pour on the chicken stock. Add the potatoes and cook until the potatoes are finished.

3. Puree the whole mixture with a hand mixer. Stir in the white wine, mustard, and crème fraîche. Then season the soup with nutmeg, salt, and pepper.

4. Cut the salmon into strips. Serve the soup in bowls with the salmon on top.

Salmon Mustard Soup

Recipes with Prepared Mustard

Ingredients

2 1/4 lbs (1kg) potatoes
1/2 lb (250g) bacon
1 bunch radishes
1 bunch parsley
1 salad cucumber
2/3 cup (150ml) chicken stock
2 Tbsp mustard
1 tsp mustard meal
Salt

Preparation

1. Wash the potatoes and cook unpeeled.

2. Cut the bacon into small squares. Wash and clean the radishes, cut off the greens, and slice. Rinse the parsley, shake dry, and chop. Cut the cucumber into slices.

3. When the potatoes are finished, drain off the water, let them cool, and then peel them and cut them carefully into slices.

4. Fry the bacon in a pan until brown.

5. Heat the stock a bit and add the mustard meal to it. Add the bacon and the prepared mustard and season with salt.

6. Mix the potatoes in with the radishes, cucumber, and parsley. Pour the stock over them and let stand a while before serving.

Piquant Potato Salad

Recipes with Prepared Mustard

Ingredients

2 1/4 lbs (1kg) ground beef
2 stale rolls
1 onion
3 eggs
1 1/3 lbs (600g) mushrooms*
2 1/4 lbs (1kg) potatoes
2 1/2 cups (300g) crème fraîche
3 Tbsp spicy mustard
2 Tbsp dried marjoram
1 bunch parsley
1 Tbsp mustard meal
1 Tbsp curry powder
1 Tbsp butter
Salt and pepper

Preparation

1. Soften the rolls in water about 3 minutes, then remove and squeeze. Peel and dice the onion. Steam and chop the parsley. Clean the mushrooms and cut into slices. Peel the potatoes and slice thin with a mandolin. Preheat the oven to 350°F (180°C).

2. Grease a casserole dish. Mix the ground beef with the rolls, onion, eggs, herbs, mustard meal, and curry. Season strongly with salt and pepper.

3. Make thin, alternating layers of the potatoes, meat, and mushrooms in the casserole dish. Top with potatoes.

4. Season the crème fraîche with the prepared mustard, salt, and pepper and spread on the top layer of potatoes. Cook covered for an hour at 350°F (180°C), then remove the lid and cook another half hour, until the surface begins to turn brown.

* Try champignon mushrooms (9 cups sliced).

Potato and Ground Beef Casserole

Recipes with Prepared Mustard

Ingredients

8 eggs
3 Tbsp wine vinegar
~6 cups (1 1/2l) water
1 1/3 Tbsp (20g) butter
1/4 cup (20g) flour
2 cups (500ml) chicken stock
1 Tbsp medium spicy mustard
1 Tbsp spicy mustard
Salt and pepper

Preparation

1. Melt the butter in a pot, sprinkle in the flour, and warm it. Stir in the stock, bring to a boil, and season with the mustard, salt, and pepper.

2. Bring about 6 cups (1 1/2l) water to a boil and add the vinegar. Break the eggs into a ladle or spoon one at a time. Slide each egg into the slightly boiling water. Poach the eggs in the boiling water 3-4 minutes each. Take the eggs out of the water with a slotted spoon and let them dry on a paper towels or in a sieve.

3. Serve the eggs with the mustard sauce soon after removing them from the water.

Salted potatoes are a good side dish.

Poached Eggs in Mustard Sauce

Recipes with Prepared Mustard

Ingredients

1 1/2 lbs (700g) potatoes
4 chicken breast fillets
2 balls mozzarella cheese
1 can diced tomatoes
4 fresh tomatoes
2 Tbsp olive oil
1 bunch basil
2 cloves garlic
1 onion
1 tsp mustard meal
3 Tbsp coarse mustard
Salt

Preparation

1. Wash the potatoes and cook about 20 minutes. Peel and cut into slices to serve with the chicken.

2. While the potatoes are cooking, peel the onion and garlic and dice small. Cut the mozzarella into slices. Wash the tomatoes and cut into 3/8-inch (1cm) cubes. Rinse the basil, shake dry, pick off leaves, and chiffonade with a sharp knife.

3. Rinse the chicken fillets and pat dry with a paper towel.

4. Heat the olive oil in a pan and fry the chicken fillets 5 minutes on each side. Take the fillets out of the pan and put aside. Fry the garlic and onion in the pan. Add the fresh and canned tomato pieces, the mustard meal, and the basil. Cook everything about 5 minutes and season with salt and mustard.

5. Coat the chicken fillets with the coarse mustard and cover with the sauce. Divide the mozzarella on the fillets and cover the pan with a lid. Heat about 5 minutes, until the mozzarella has melted.

Chicken Fillets Topped with Mozzarella

Recipes with Prepared Mustard

Ingredients

4 Belgian endive hearts
1 Tbsp sugar
1 Tbsp olive oil
3 pears
3/8 cup (100ml) white wine
6 slices toast
7/8 cup (100g) pine nuts
1 tsp mustard meal
3/8 cup (100ml) sweet cream
3 Tbsp coarse mustard
3 1/2 oz (100g) blue cheese, ~3/4 cup crumbled
Salt and pepper

Preparation

1. Wash and quarter the endive. Cut the toast into cubes 3/8 inch (1cm) thick. Peel the pears, remove the cores, and cube the fruit. Stir the mustard meal and the coarse mustard into the cream.

2. Fry the pine nuts in a pan without fat. Remove the nuts and fry the bread cubes.

3. Cook the pears in the wine about 10 minutes. When the pears are soft, stir in the cream and mustard mixture and season with salt and pepper.

4. Heat the olive oil in a pan, sprinkle in the sugar and stir until it has melted. Fry the endive on all sides.

5. Crumble the blue cheese and add to the pear sauce. Put the endive on plates and serve with the pear and mustard sauce.

Warm Endive and Pear Salad with Mustard Dressing

Recipes with Prepared Mustard

Ingredients

4 pork cutlets
2 Tbsp spicy mustard
1 cup (100g) flour
3 Tbsp whipping cream
1 tsp mustard meal
3 eggs
1 2/3 cups (200g) breadcrumbs
Frying fat
Salt and pepper

Preparation

1. Divide the pork cutlets into four small pieces each, salt, pepper, and coat heavily with the prepared mustard on both sides.
2. Break the eggs, beat, and mix with the mustard meal and cream. Put the flour, the egg and cream mixture, and the breadcrumbs on three separate plates. Coat the cutlets successively with the flour, the egg, and the breadcrumbs.
3. Heat the frying fat in a pan and fry the cutlets a golden brown on both sides over medium heat.

The cutlets can be served hot or cold. The spicy potato salad on page 22 makes a splendid side dish.

Mustard Schnitzel

Recipes with Prepared Mustard

Ingredients

4 chicken breast fillets
1 tsp mustard meal
1 tsp starch
2 Tbsp olive oil
1/2 lb (250g) fresh mushrooms*, 3 1/3 cup chopped
1 fresh pineapple
1/2 lb (200g) asparagus
1/3 cup (70ml) chicken stock
2 Tbsp spicy mustard
1 tsp curry powder
Salt and pepper

Preparation

1. Wash the chicken fillets, brush off the water, and cut the meat into strips. Put the meat in a bowl, mix with the oil, mustard meal, and starch—season with salt. Let it marinade about an hour.

2. Clean the mushrooms and cut into pieces. Peel the pineapple and cut into cubes. Peel the asparagus and cut into 3/4-inch (2cm) pieces.

3. Put the chicken in a pot and fry thoroughly. Pour on the chicken stock. Add the mushrooms, pineapple, and asparagus and let it heat about 10 minutes.

4. Season it with mustard, curry powder, salt, and pepper.

* Try champignon mushrooms. This dish also goes very well with barley.

Exotic Mustard Curry

Recipes with Prepared Mustard

Ingredients

4 steaks, pounded into thin roulades
4 slices ham, thin
10-oz package of spinach (200g)
2 Tbsp coarse mustard
2 Tbsp frying fat
1 carrot
1 leek
1 bunch mixed herbs
2 slices (50g) pumpernickel bread
1 2/3 cups (400ml) water
1 tsp mustard meal
Salt and pepper

Preparation

1. Clean and wash the spinach and blanch briefly in boiling water. Take it out of the water and separate the leaves. Preheat the oven to 350°F (180°C)

2. Clean the carrot and leek and cut up coarsely. Rinse the herbs.

3. Spread out the roulades on a cutting board, brush with coarse mustard, and add the ham. Put the spinach leaves on top of the ham. Now roll the roulades tightly and secure with string. Season the outside with salt and pepper.

4. Heat the fat in an oven-safe pan and brown the roulades on all sides. Add the vegetables, bread, and herbs and fill up with water. Bake the roulades in the oven for about an hour at 350°F (180°C).

5. Take the meat out of the pan and pour the sauce through a sieve into another pot. Add the mustard meal and season the sauce with salt and pepper.

6. Serve the roulades on noodles.

Piquant Beef Roulade

Recipes with Prepared Mustard

Ingredients

1 cup (200g) rice
8 red peppers
1 lb (400g) ground beef
1 onion
2 cloves garlic
1 Tbsp olive oil
1 tsp mustard meal
2 Tbsp butter
2 Tbsp flour
7/8 cup (200ml) chicken stock
1 Tbsp spicy mustard
Salt and pepper

Preparation

1. Cook the rice according to the instructions on the package and then drain if necessary.
2. Peel the onion and garlic and dice small. Cut the tops off the peppers and carefully remove the core.
3. Heat the oil in a pan and brown the ground beef in it. When it is light brown, add the onion and garlic and cook until the onions turn translucent. Mix the meat with the mustard meal and the rice; season with salt and pepper. Stuff the mixture into the red peppers.
4. Heat the butter in a pot and brown the stuffed peppers on all sides. Pour on the chicken stock and let it cook about 15 minutes.
5. Take the peppers out of the stock and keep warm. Make a roux with the flour and some stock from the pot and thicken the remaining broth. Bring it to a boil, stir in the mustard, and season the sauce with salt and pepper.

Stuffed Peppers with Mustard Sauce

Recipes with Prepared Mustard

Ingredients

1 1/2 lbs (700g) beef heart
1 onion
1 bunch pearl onions
2 Tbsp frying fat
3/8 cup (100ml) beef stock

1 cup sour cream
1 Tbsp spicy mustard
1 Tbsp coarse sweet mustard
Salt and pepper

Preparation

1. Cut the beef heart into cubes, removing any fat or tendons. Clean the pearl onions and cut into pieces. Peel them and chop them small.

2. Heat the frying fat in a pan and fry the heart pieces for about 10 minutes. Add the onion pieces, fry briefly, then add the stock and cook another 10 minutes.

3. Stir in the cream, mustard, and pearl onions. Season with salt and pepper.

Serve the beef heart over noodles.

Beef Heart in Creamy Mustard Sauce

Recipes with Prepared Mustard

Ingredients

- 1 1/3 lbs (600g) zucchini, 5 1/3 cups sliced
- 1 onion
- 2 cloves garlic
- 2 Tbsp olive oil
- 2 cups (500ml) lively white wine*
- 3 egg yolks
- 2 Tbsp medium spicy mustard
- Salt and pepper

Preparation

1. Wash the zucchini and cut into slices. Peel the onion and garlic and dice small.

2. Heat the olive oil in a pot and brown the onion and garlic. Add the zucchini slices and fry until the slices turn a little brown. Pour in 2-3 tablespoons of water and cook until the zucchini is done.

3. To make the sabayon, put some water in the bottom of a double boiler and heat. If a double boiler is not available, heat the water in a regular pot and set a bowl slightly larger than the pot on top, making sure that the bottom of the bowl does not come in contact with the water.

4. Put the egg yolks in the top of the double boiler, or a bowl, and stir constantly with a whisk. The eggs must get warm but not hot. Add the white wine and mustard until the mixture has tripled in quantity. The sauce will thicken as you continue to whisk. Season the finished sauce with salt and pepper.

5. Plate the zucchini and pour the mustard sabayon on top.

* Try a chardonnay or white pinot noir.

Zucchini with Mustard Sabayon

Recipes with Prepared Mustard

Ingredients

1 large rainbow trout
1 bunch dill
3/4 cup (150g) sugar
1/3 cup (100g) salt
1 Tbsp coriander seeds
2 Tbsp white mustard seeds
1 tsp white pepper

For the Sauce:
3 Tbsp wild honey
3 Tbsp medium spicy mustard
1 tsp white mustard seeds
1 tsp pink peppercorns
1/2 bunch dill
Salt and pepper

Preparation

1. Wash, clean, and fillet the trout, but do not skin it! Remove all bones and put the fillets in the refrigerator.

2. Wash the dill, shake it out, and chop coarsely. Crush the coriander and mustard seeds with a wide knife, then mix the sugar, salt, dill, pepper, coriander, and mustard seeds.

3. Put a sufficiently large sheet of aluminum foil on a platter and put some of the spice mixture on the foil. Lay half the trout on it with the skin side down. Apply more of the spices to the fillet, put the second fillet on top of it, and put the rest of the mixture on it. Wrap the fish firmly with the foil. Put the fish in a cool place for two or three days (if you have no such place, use the refrigerator). Pour off the juice from it now and then.

4. Crush the pink peppercorn and mustard seeds. Rinse the dill, shake it dry, pick the leaves off the stems, and cut up with a sharp knife. Mix the honey with the mustard and add the crushed mustard and peppercorns with the dill. Season the sauce with salt and pepper.

To serve, cut the trout into thin slices with a sharp knife. You can also use this recipe with a whole salmon. Simply halve the salmon in the middle and follow the recipe.

Cured Trout with Honey Mustard Sauce

Recipes with Prepared Mustard

Ingredients

10 eggs
2 Tbsp mayonnaise
2 Tbsp medium spicy mustard
Cream
Salt and pepper

For the Garnish:
Radishes
Chives
Coarse mustard
Coarse paprika powder
Fish roe

Preparation

1. Cook the eggs 10 minutes. Remove the eggshells and halve the eggs with a sharp knife. Take out the yolks and put them in a bowl. Put the empty egg halves on a plate.

2. Add the mayonnaise and mustard to the egg yolks. Mix them to a creamy consistency with a whisk. If the mixture is too stiff, add 1 or 2 tablespoons of cream. Season the yolks with salt and pepper.

3. Put the yolk mixture into a piping bag and fill the egg halves with it.

4. Garnish the filled eggs with radishes, chives, coarse mustard, coarse paprika powder, and fish roe.

Deviled Eggs

Recipes with Prepared Mustard

Ingredients

2/3 lb (300g) bologna (Fleischwurst)
2/3 lb (300g) blood pudding (Blutwurst)*
1/2 lb (200g) Swiss cheese
1/3 lb (150g) cocktail tomatoes
1 head lettuce
1 cup sour cream
2 Tbsp coarse mustard
1 tsp sugar
1 Tbsp wine vinegar
Salt and pepper

Preparation

1. Cut the Blutwurst and other cold cuts into bite-size pieces. Cut the cheese into strips. Halve the cocktail tomatoes, quarter the larger ones. Wash the lettuce and let it drip dry.
2. Mix sausage, cheese, and tomato.
3. Put the sour cream in a bowl, mix in the mustard, vinegar, and sugar. Season the sauce with salt and pepper.
4. Plate the salad vegetables, add the meat and cheese mixture, and pour the dressing on top.

* Use other types of deli sausages if Blutwurst isn't available.

Chef's Salad with Mustard Dressing

Recipes with Prepared Mustard

Ingredients

1 3/4 lbs (800g) fish fillet*
Juice of 1/2 lemon
3 Tbsp medium spicy mustard
2 onions
4 beefsteak tomatoes
1 each red, yellow, and green peppers
1 Tbsp butter
1 bunch mixed herbs
2 eggs
1/3 cup (100g) sweet cream
7/8 cup (100g) crème fraîche
1 tsp mustard meal
7/8 cup (100g) grated cheese
Salt and pepper

Preparation

1. Wash the fish fillets and pat dry. Press the lemon, pour the juice on the fillets, and then coat with mustard. Preheat the oven to 350°F (180°C).

2. Peel the onions and cut into thin rings. Wash the tomatoes, cut an "X" into the bottoms, and pour boiling water over them. Peel them and cut them into slices. Wash the peppers, halve them and remove the stems, seeds, and membrane. Cut into strips.

3. Grease a casserole pan with butter and put the fillets in. Cover the fish with the vegetables.

4. Wash the herbs and shake dry. Remove the leaves and chop them small. Mix the eggs, cream, crème fraîche, mustard meal, and chopped herbs. Season strongly with salt and pepper. Pour the mixture over the vegetables. Sprinkle grated cheese on top.

5. Put the casserole pan in an oven preheated to 350°F (180°C) and bake for about an hour.

* Recommended fish are cod, perch, or sea salmon

Fish Casserole

Recipes with Prepared Mustard

Ingredients

4 cod fillets
1 lemon
3 Tbsp coarse mustard
1 bunch mixed herbs
7/8 cup (100g) grated cheese
2 1/4 lbs (1kg) fresh spinach
Nutmeg
Salt and pepper

Preparation

1. Wash the fish fillets and pat dry. Make zest of the lemon rind, squeeze the lemon, and pour the juice on the fish. Preheat the oven to 350°F (180°C).

2. Rinse the herbs, shake them dry, chop them small, and put them in a bowl. Mix in the lemon zest, cheese, and mustard. Season with salt and pepper.

3. Clean and wash the spinach and put right into a heated pot of water. Stir until it becomes tender and collapses. Season the spinach with nutmeg, salt, and pepper.

4. Divide the herb and cheese mixture on the cod fillets. Put the spinach in a casserole dish, put the fillets on top, and bake about 10 minutes in an oven preheated to 350°F (180°C).

Serve with potatoes.

Cod with Herb Mustard Crust

Recipes with Prepared Mustard

Ingredients

4 trout
2 cloves garlic
1 bunch parsley
1 Tbsp mustard seeds
4 Tbsp medium spicy mustard
4 Tbsp flour
2 Tbsp butter
1 lemon
Dill sprigs
Salt and pepper

Preparation

1. Wash the trout under running water and let drip dry.

2. Peel the garlic and dice fine. Rinse the parsley, chop coarse, and put in a bowl. Mix the parsley, garlic, mustard seeds, and 2 tablespoons of mustard. Stuff the trout with this mixture.

3. Coat the trout with the remaining mustard and roll in flour.

4. Melt the butter in a pan and fry the trout slowly in it over low heat. When the trout are brown, take them from the pan and plate them. Garnish with lemon slices and dill and serve with potato salad.

Stuffed Trout

Recipes with Prepared Mustard

Ingredients

3 medium-sized fresh eels
1 bunch celery stalks
4 large carrots (300g)
1 onion
1 1/4 cups (300ml) dry white wine
1 Tbsp mustard seeds
2 Tbsp strong mustard
Salt and pepper

Preparation

1. Prepare the eel for cooking and cut into pieces. Clean and wash the celery and cut into 1/8-inch (1/2cm) pieces. Peel the carrots and cut into sticks. Peel the onion and dice fine.

2. Heat the oil in a pot. Brown the onion and vegetables. Pour on the white wine, add the mustard seeds, put the eel pieces on the vegetables, and cook covered about 10 minutes.

3. Take the eel pieces out of the pot, stir the mustard into the vegetables, and season with salt and pepper.

4. Plate the vegetables with the eel pieces on top and serve with potatoes.

To prepare the eel:
Wash the eel and clean the intestinal cavity. Then, with a sharp knife, just behind the first fin, cut into the skin all the way around. Loosen the skin somewhat with your fingers and then pull it off the length of the whole eel in one motion.

Eel with Vegetables in Mustard Sauce

Cooking with Whole Mustard Seeds

Ingredients

2 onions
1 each, leek and carrot
1/2 bunch celery
1 tsp black peppercorns
1 Tbsp white mustard seeds
1/4 lb (100g) soup bone
1 lb (400g) meat, for soup
1 3/4 cups (175g) flour
2 eggs
1 tsp mustard meal
4 potatoes
1/2 bunch parsley
2 Tbsp butter
Salt and pepper

Preparation

1. Peel and halve an onion. Clean and wash the leek and cut into 2 or 3 pieces. Peel the carrot and celery, wash, and cut into pieces. Wash and peel the potatoes and cut into pieces.
2. Bring the vegetables, mustard, pepper, 1 teaspoon salt, the soup meat (whole), and bone to a boil in a stock pot with 8 cups (2l) water. Reduce the heat and simmer for two hours.
3. Stir the flour, eggs, 1 teaspoon salt, the mustard meal, and 7/8 cup (200ml) water into a dough. Put the dough in a spätzle maker and cut the noodles directly into boiling water. Take the noodles out after two or three minutes and let them dry.
4. Take the meat out of the stock and put it aside. Strain the broth through a sieve and save it. Discard the vegetables and soup bone. Bring the broth to a boil and cook the potatoes in it until done.
5. Meanwhile, cut the meat into cubes. Wash the parsley, shake dry, and chop. Peel the other onions and cut into rings. Melt the butter in a pan and brown the onion rings.
6. Add the meat, noodles, and parsley to the potatoes in the broth. Season the soup with mustard, salt, and pepper and serve with the onion rings.

Tasty Spätzle Soup

Cooking with Whole Mustard Seeds

Ingredients

10 large carrots (700g)
1 bunch coriander
3/8 cup (100ml) water
1/2 tsp mustard meal
3 Tbsp mustard seeds
1/3 cup (100g) butter
1 Tbsp olive oil
1 pinch sugar
Salt and pepper

Preparation

1. Peel the carrots and cut into thin slices. Rinse the coriander, shake dry, pick the leaves from the stems, and chop.

2. Heat the olive oil in a pan and sauté the carrots.

3. Pour the mustard meal and water in with the carrots and cook about 15 minutes. Stir 2/3 of the coriander into the carrots and season with salt, sugar, and pepper.

4. Melt the butter in a pot until a foam forms and the butter hisses. Remove the foam with a spoon. Put the mustard seeds in the butter and roast about 10 minutes. Add the rest of the coriander, stir, and serve the mustard butter along with the carrots.

Carrots in Mustard Butter

Cooking with Whole Mustard Seeds

Ingredients

1 2/3 lbs (750g) fruit (mango, apple, pear, pineapple, banana, etc.)
2 Tbsp mustard seeds
1 tsp mustard meal
2/3 cup (150ml) water
1/3 cup (80ml) fruit vinegar
2 cups (400g) brown sugar
4 beefsteaks
1 tsp honey
1 tsp Sambal Oelek (Asian chili sauce)
2 Tbsp frying fat
Salt and pepper

Preparation

1. Boil the water with the vinegar, sugar, mustard seeds, and mustard meal.

2. Wash the fruit and cut into bite-size chunks. Pour the above mixture over the fruit while it is still hot. Let the fruit marinade for about two hours.

3. Make a paste of the honey, mustard seeds, Sambal Oelek, salt, and pepper. Rub it on the edges of the steaks. Heat the frying fat in a pan and fry the steaks in it about 4 minutes on each side.

4. Serve the mustard fruit along with the steaks.

Spicy Steak with Sweet and Savory Fruit

Recipes with Mustard Meal

Ingredients

1 1/8 lbs (500g) pork belly
4 cups (1l) water
1 tsp mustard seeds
1 bay leaf
2 cloves
3 allspice berries
1 tsp peppercorns
1/2 lb (200g) green beans
1/2 lb (200g) carrots
1 tsp mustard meal
2 stalks lovage
Salt and pepper

Preparation

1. Put the pork belly in a pot of water.
2. Add the mustard seeds, allspice, and peppercorns. Cook the meat about an hour.
3. Clean the beans and cut them. Peel the carrots and cut into bite-size chunks.
4. Take the meat out of the pot and cut into cubes. Pour the stock through a sieve into another pot. Add the beans and carrots and cook about 10 minutes. Shortly before the vegetables are done, add the lovage, stir in the mustard meal, and season the soup with salt and pepper.
5. Add the meat to the soup and serve.

Pork Belly and Vegetable Soup

Recipes with Mustard Meal

Ingredients

2 1/4 lbs (1kg) potatoes
2/3 cup (150ml) milk
1/2 tsp mustard meal
1 egg yolk
1 endive head
1/2 lb (200g) bacon
1 Tbsp oil
1 Tbsp medium spicy mustard
2 Tbsp sugar
1/3 cup (70ml) balsamic vinegar
Nutmeg
Salt and pepper

Preparation

1. Peel the potatoes and cook in salt water. Warm the milk in a pot (but do not bring to a boil), add the egg yolk and mustard meal. Season the milk strongly with salt, pepper, and nutmeg.

2. Wash the lettuce and cut into strips. Cut the bacon into small cubes.

3. Heat the oil in a pan and fry the bacon in it. When it is brown, sprinkle the sugar over it and stir until it has melted. Pour the vinegar over the bacon and season with pepper.

4. Drain the potatoes and mash to a puree with the milk mixture; season with salt, pepper, and nutmeg. Plate the mashed potatoes, cover with the salad, and top with the bacon sauce.

Mashed Potatoes and Salad with Bacon Mustard Dressing

Recipes with Mustard Meal

Ingredients

1 1/8 lbs (500g) green beans
8 cups (2l) water
1 2/3 lbs (750g) lamb meat
4 Tbsp olive oil
2 onions
2 potatoes
2 each, carrots and leeks
4 Tbsp butter
4 cups (1l) meat stock
1 tsp mustard meal
Some marjoram
1 Tbsp medium spicy mustard
1/2 Tbsp vinegar
Salt and pepper

Preparation

1. Wash and clean the beans and blanch about 3 minutes in boiling salt water. Drain the beans, rinse with cold water, and put aside.

2. Wash, dry, and cube the meat. Peel the onions and dice fine. Peel and cube the potatoes and carrots. Trim the leeks, halve lengthwise, wash thoroughly, and cut in rings.

3. Heat the oil in a pan and brown the meat cubes in it.

4. Melt the butter in a wide pot and gradually add the onions, leeks, carrots, and potatoes. Sauté and season with marjoram.

5. Add the meat to the vegetables in the pot and stir well. Then add the beans to the mixture and stir again.

6. Pour on the meat stock, add the mustard meal, cover, and cook 30-40 minutes until the meat is soft. Season with mustard, vinegar, salt and pepper.

Lamb and Green Bean Stew

Recipes with Mustard Meal

Ingredients

8 pickled herring fillets
1 bunch pearl onions
2 red peppers
1 tsp mustard meal
1 cup crème fraîche
1 Tbsp sugar
2 Tbsp white wine vinegar
Salt

Preparation

1. Cut the herring fillets into medium-sized pieces. Clean the pearl onions and cut into rings. Wash the red peppers, halve, remove the seeds, and dice. Put everything into a bowl and mix well.

2. Put the crème fraîche into a bowl, stir in the mustard meal, sugar, and vinegar. Season with salt.

3. Plate the salad and serve dressed with the mustard sauce.

Here is an alternative sauce for this salad:

3 Tbsp low-fat mayonnaise
1 Tbsp whole white mustard seeds
2 Tbsp sweet cream
1 tsp sugar
1 pinch salt

Mix everything well and let sit for about an hour.

Herring Salad

Recipes with Mustard Meal

Ingredients

- 28 oz (800g) rigatoni (~2, 16-oz boxes)
- 1 1/3 lbs (600g) cooked ham
- 1 lb (400g) Gouda cheese, 3 1/2 cups grated
- 7 eggs
- 1 tsp mustard meal
- 2 Tbsp mustard
- 1 bunch basil
- 1 Tbsp butter
- Salt and pepper

Preparation

1. Preheat the oven to 350°F (180°C). Cook the noodles in heavily salted water until ready to eat.

2. Cube the ham, rinse the basil, pick the leaves off the stems, and chiffonade.

3. Beat the eggs in a bowl, mix in the ham, basil, mustard meal, mustard, and half the cheese; season strongly with salt and pepper.

4. Mix the noodles with the egg and ham mixture. Grease a casserole dish with butter, put the noodles in, cover, and cook in the oven about 15 minutes at 350°F (180°C). Remove the cover, add the rest of the cheese, and leave in the oven uncovered another 7 minutes until the cheese is golden brown.

Rigatoni al Forno

Recipes with Mustard Meal

Ingredients

1 1/8 lbs (500g) ground beef
1 onion
1 egg
2 Tbsp coarse sweet mustard
1 bunch parsley
2 Tbsp breadcrumbs
2 Tbsp vegetable oil
2 bunches Swiss chard
3 1/3 Tbsp (50ml) water
1 cup crème fraîche
1 Tbsp mustard meal
Salt and pepper

Preparation

1. Peel the onion and dice fine. Rinse the parsley, pick the leaves from the stems, and chop them. Wash the Swiss chard, cut the leaves into strips and the stems into thin pieces.

2. Put the ground beef in a bowl and mix with the onion, egg, breadcrumbs, parsley, and mustard. Season with salt and pepper. Make meatballs with the mixture.

3. Heat the oil in a pan and brown the meatballs.

4. Put the chard and the water in a pot and steam about 8 minutes over low heat. Stir in the crème fraîche with the mustard meal and season with salt and pepper.

5. Serve the meatballs over the chard.

Meatballs over Swiss Chard in Mustard Sauce

Recipes with Mustard Meal

Ingredients

8 smoked trout fillets
1 head lettuce
1 cup crème fraîche
1 Tbsp creamy horseradish
1 tsp mustard meal
Salt and pepper

Preparation

1. Remove the lettuce stalk and wash the leaves in cold water. Let them drip dry and then cut into 1/8 inch (1/2cm) wide strips.
2. Mix the cream with the creamy horseradish and mustard meal. Let the sauce set a bit to build up the necessary spiciness. Season the sauce with salt and pepper.
3. Plate the salad, top with two trout fillets, and serve dressed with the horseradish and mustard sauce.

This mustard sauce also goes well with other smoked fish, such as mackerel, eel, dogfish, etc.

Smoked Trout with Horseradish Mustard Sauce

Recipes with Mustard Meal

Ingredients

3 cups (300g) flour
2, 5/16 oz packages yeast (20g)
1/2 cup (1/8l) milk
1 Tbsp mustard meal
1/2 cup (100g) butter
4 eggs
3 1/3 lbs (1 1/2kg) onions
1/8 lb (50g) smoked bacon
1 2/3 cup (200g) sour cream
2 Tbsp spicy mustard
1 tsp cumin
Salt
Butter for greasing pan

Preparation

1. Sift the flour into a bowl and make a well in the middle. Crumble the yeast into half the milk heated to lukewarm. Pour the milk and yeast into the well. Mix into a dough. Cover and put in a warm place for 20 minutes. Preheat the oven to 350°F (180°C).

2. Add small flakes of butter, an egg, the mustard meal, and a pinch of salt to the dough. Knead everything together. Gradually add the rest of the milk until a smooth dough results. Cover and let it rise 30 minutes.

3. Peel the onions and cut into rings. Melt the butter in a pot and sauté the onions in it over low heat until they are translucent.

4. Cube the bacon and fry it crispy without fat. Stir the rest of the eggs, cream, mustard, a pinch of salt, and the cumin in with the bacon. Fold in the onions.

5. Knead the dough forcefully and make a ball of it. Roll it into a circle and lay it into a greased spring form. Raise the edge of the dough, press it into the corners of the form, and perforate the dough several times with a fork. Spoon the onion mixture into the form and bake the resulting pie about 40-50 minutes in the oven at 350°F (180°C).

6. Remove the quiche from the spring form, cut into slices, and serve warm.

Onion Quiche

Register